THE SURVEY OF AMERICAN COLLEGE STUDENTS: Student Use of Library E-book Collections

ISBN #: 1-57440-113-0

METHODOLOGY

The Survey of American College Students is a stratified, representative probability study of full time college students in the United States. Participants were chosen from a representative initial sample base of approximately 250 colleges in the United States. Students were chosen randomly within pre-determined segments. The sample was stratified into three segments, and each segment was separately sampled. The three segments were: Public 4-year colleges, Private Four Year Colleges, and Public and Private Two Year Colleges. The weights for the three segments were established using data from the U.S. Department of Education's Center for Education Statistics. A sample of students was sent a postcard directing them to an online survey site. Safeguards insured that only invitees could take the survey; some allowances in the survey strategy were made to account for response variations caused by divergent reactions to survey incentives offered and other factors that can cause higher response rates from some population segments than others.

THE UNIVERSE FROM WHICH THE SAMPLE IS DRAWN DOES NOT INCLUDE:

Graduate & Professional School Students
Part Time College Students, Graduate or Undergraduate
Students Studying Overseas but who are officially enrolled in U.S. colleges at the time
Canadian college students
Students of For-Profit Colleges* (about 7.5% of U.S. full time college students)

*The lists that we use to compile a universe from which to sample do not at this time include students of for-profit colleges.

THE UNIVERSE FROM WHICH THE SAMPLE IS DRAWN DOES INCLUDE:

Full Time Community College Students
Full Time Private College Students
Full Time Public College Students
Full Time Foreign Students studying at U.S. Colleges

THE TOTAL SAMPLE SIZE WAS 407.

In the subcategories, the cells containing data for students living in fraternities and sororities, the cells for students who are very left wing or very right wing and the cell for students with D grade averages are very small, less than a fifth the size of the smallest cell. These cells are too small for highly accurate results but we have presented them in any case because, generally, they are nonetheless often representative and capture obvious trends if not subtleties. Nonetheless the data in these 4 cells should be viewed with some caution.   Typical cells have data for between 60 to 250 survey participants with a general average of about 100.

HOW TO READ THE DATA

The Survey of American College Students is a series of 18 reports on various aspects of the American college student experience. The overall series has three types of tables and most reports have at least two of the three types and some have all three.

The three types of fundamental tables are "Yes/No", Multiple Choice, and Open Ended Data Questions. Results are presented in one table for the entire sample and then in s long series of tables for the sample broken out by numerous criteria. Below is a sample table taken from one of the reports in this series.

YES/NO Questions. Typically, in these questions, students are asked if they have done or experienced something, in this case, if they ever reported an incident to the campus police, and the table relates the percentage who have or have not done so.

Percentage of Full Time College Students Who Have Ever Reported an Incident to the Campus Police, Broken Out by Income Level of the Student's Family of Origin*

Annual Income of Student's Family of Origin	Yes	No
Less than $40,000	5.96%	94.04%
$40,00 to $75,000	9.52%	90.48%
$75,000+ to $150,000	16.67%	83.33%
More than $150,000	17.07%	82.93%

*Current Family Status for Students Over 40 Years of Age

The first part of the heading – "Percentage of Full Time College Students Who Have Ever Reported an Incident to the Campus Police" refers to the original question posed to the student, and the second part –"Broken Out by Income Level of the Student's Family of Origin" tells you how the data is broken out, that it is broken out by categories based on the income level of the student's family or origin (or for students over 40 years of age by their own current income).

The left hand column – Annual Income of Student's Family of Origin – is the variable by which the data is being broken out. So this table breaks out by annual income level the percentage of students who have ever reported an incident to the campus police. It shows that the higher the income of the student's family of origin the more likely they are to have ever reported an incident to the campus police. Only 5.96% of students from families with incomes of less than $40,000 have ever reported an incident to the campus police while 17.07% of students with incomes of greater than $150,000 have done so.

Multiple Choice Questions

Multiple Choice questions are organized along the same lines as the Yes/No questions except that they generally involve from 3 to 6 possible answers rather than just two, yes or no. The following multiple choice question is taken from this report and presents aggregated answers to the question: How likely are you to seek out the college's tutoring services in the future? In this case the data is broken out by gender.

Likelihood that student will seek out the college tutoring service in the future, Broken Out by Gender of the Student

Gender of the Student	Highly unlikely	Unlikely	Possibly	Likely	Highly likely
Male	14.86%	22.30%	31.08%	16.89%	14.86%
Female	14.84%	19.92%	33.59%	21.09%	10.55%

Quantitative Data Question

The third type of question is an open ended quantitative data question. Students are asked: how many? How much? This particular report does not have any of this type of question but we have provided an example from another report in this series.

Mean, Median, Minimum and Maximum Number of Times in the Past Month the Student Has Been in the College Bookstore, Broken Out by Public and Private College Students

Attends Public or Private College	Mean	Median	Minimum	Maximum
Attends Public College	2.01	1.00	0.00	20.00
Attends Private College	3.10	2.00	0.00	30.00

Reading left to right in the second row shows the mean, median, minimum and maximum number of times that students attending public colleges have visited the college bookstore in the past month. The second row relates that the mean or average number of visits to the college bookstore per month for public college students was 2.01 and that the median was 1.0. The median is the number "in the middle" of all of the numbers, midway between numbers that are greater and those that are less. So if you had a series of numbers 1,2, and 9, the median would be 2, and the mean or average would be 4, or 1+2+9 divided by 3. Minimum refers to the student or students that visited the fewest number of times and Maximum refers to the student or students who visited most frequently. In the table above the public college student in the sample that visited the college bookstore the most in the past month was 20 times and, for private college students, the student that visited most went 30 times.

THE QUESTIONNAIRE

1-What do you think of your college library's E-book collection?

I am not sure what an E-book is.

I don't think that my library has an E-book collection.

My library has E-books but I never use them.

I use the library E-book collection occasionally.

I'm a frequent user of my library's E-book collection.

2-The library ebook collection is:

Very easy to access and use

Relatively easy to access and use.

Moderately difficult to access and use.

Very difficult to access and use

I'm not really sure.

3- Have you ever received any form of in or out of class training from a college librarian in how to use the college library E-book collection?

Yes

No

4- . As a reference and research tool for you how would you rate your library's E-book collection?

Not useful to me.

Slightly useful to me.

Somewhat useful to me.

 Useful to me

Very useful to me.

HOW THE DATA IS BROKEN OUT

The data gives national norms for full time college students and then breaks the data down into categories. The categories are based on size or type of college, or the habits, beliefs or demographic characteristics of the students in the sample. Some of the ways that the data are broken down are:

For public college students vs. private college students

By the age of the student

By the academic year of the student, freshmen, sophomore, junior, senior

For different size colleges defined by total FTE enrollment

By the level of degree offered by the college, i.e. community college, BA level, MA level, PHD level or major research university.

By the mean SAT score of the students that attend the college. Data is presented separately for individuals in institutions in five different SAT categories: less than 1500, 1500 to 1649, 1650 to 1799, 1800 to 1950 and Greater than 1950. (These categories are based on the published claims of the colleges attended by the students)

For men vs. women

By the type of locale, in terms of geographic area of the US or abroad, Northeast, South, Midwest, West, Abroad – where the student grew up.

Data is broken out separately for the type of locale, in terms of population intensity, of where the student grew up. Data presented for those who grew up in suburban areas, rural areas, and small and large cities.

By general academic major or main area of academic focus

For students with grade point averages in the A,B,C and D range

By lifestyle distinctions such as the level of commitment to organized religion, or by the living arrangement of the student: i.e. those living on campus, off campus, off campus alone, with parents or guardian, etc, and by the student's employment situation: those who do not work, those who work part time, and those who work full time.

TABLE OF CONTENTS

LIST OF TABLES

SUMMARY OF MAIN FINDINGS

Level of Awareness & Use of E-books in the Student Population

Close to a third of the students in the sample were not sure what an E-book was and another 9.5% believed that their library did not have an E-book collection. Another 27.25% said that their library had an E-book collection but that they never used them. 27% of the students in the sample said that they used the E-book collection occasionally and 4% said that they were frequent users of their library's E-book collection.

Interestingly almost all of the frequent users of college library E-book collections were students 21 years of age or younger, suggesting that E-book use is such a new phenomena that even older current students have not developed the habit as much as slightly younger current students. There is literally a "generational gap" in E-book use between the 22 year olds and the 20 year olds.

Southerners and Northeasterners were more likely than others to now know what an E-book was and students in the West were the most likely to be frequent E-book users. All frequent users of E-books in the sample were A or B students; two thirds of students with C averages did not think that their colleges had E-book collections.

The hard sciences had the fewest number of frequent E-book collection users, only 1.35% of students pursuing majors or concentrations in this area were frequent E-book users. Students in Education and English/Communications/Languages/Journalism were the heaviest users. Students in private colleges and women tended to be heavier users than students in public colleges or men.

No student with a full time job in the sample was a frequent user and this is certainly a shame since in many respects E-books are ideal for students without time to actually go to and from the library. Students in institutions granting PhD's but that were not research universities had the highest percentage of frequent users. However, no student at any institution with a mean SAT acceptance score of greater than 1800 was a frequent user of E-books. It was the middle to upper-middle level college (in terms of SAT acceptance scores) that accounted for the highest percentage of E-book frequent users; 8.33% of students in colleges with a mean SAT acceptance range of 1650 to 1799 were frequent E-book users.

Perception of the Ease of Use of E-Book Collections

Far more students thought that the library's E-book collection was easy or relatively easy to use than thought it moderately difficult or very difficult to use. However, more than 55% were not sure presumably because they had not tried their college's E-book collection of their college did not have onc.

Students from lower income backgrounds were somewhat less aware of E-books than were students from wealthier backgrounds. Close to 58% of students from families with annual incomes of less than $75,000 were unsure of the accessibility and ease of use of their college E-book collections while this was true for about 42% of students from families with annual incomes of greater than $75,000. All students who found E-book collections very easy to access and use averaged B- or better. No students with grades in the C or D range found E-books very easy to access and use. Lack of awareness of E-books rose as grades fell.

Oddly, those students who were relatively unlikely to use E-books, such as those in the hard sciences and social sciences, had the highest percentages of students who found them easy to access and to use. Students in private colleges were slightly more likely to find E-book collections easy to use than were students from public colleges though the differences were modest.

Percentage of Students Who Have Received Training from a College Librarian in the Use of the E-Book Collection

30.42% of the students in the sample say that they have received any form of in or out of class training from a college librarian in how to use the library's E-book collection. Students in the 20-21 year old age range have received such training slightly more often than older or younger students perhaps reflecting the recent addition of E-book collection training to information literacy training efforts. All students who say that they have received such training were students with average grades in the A or B range. No student in the C or D grade range say that they have received any form of E-book collection training or, if they did, it does not seem to have made a lasting impression. Half of all students majoring or having a concentration in language oriented programs such as English/Communications/Languages or Journalism say that they have had some form of E-book collection training from college librarians in some capacity.

40% of private college students say that they have had such training, while 26.55% of public college student say so. Not a single student with a full time job says that they have received training in how to use the library's E-book collection. Only a sixth of students in colleges with a mean SAT score greater than 1950 say that they have received E-book collection training from college librarians.

Student Evaluation of the Usefulness of the E-Book Collection

Only 3.69% of the students in the sample say that the college E-book collection is "very useful to me" as a reference or research tool. Another 21.31% say that it is "useful to me" and another 24.43% say that it is "somewhat useful to me" while 17.05% say that the collections are "slightly useful to me" and 33.52% say that they are "not useful to me".

Students from middle-upper and upper income families are more likely than lower income students to consider the collections useful or very useful. Students in the fine or performing arts were the least likely to find the collections useful or very useful while those in social sciences and English and other language oriented majors were most likely to find them useful or very useful. Private college students were more likely than public college students to find them useful or very useful. No student with a full time job found them useful, very useful or even somewhat useful. Once again, this is disconcerting since these students might benefit the most from use of E-book collections since time constraints are greatest for them.

Less than 17% of community college students found library E-book collections useful or very useful while more than 28% of research university students found them to be useful to very useful.

QUESTION #1: Student Opinions of College Library E-book Collections

Table 1.1: Students' opinion of college library's E-book collection

	I am not sure what an E-book is.	I don't think that my library has an E-book collection.	My library has E-books but I never use them.	I use the library E-book collection occasionally.	I'm a frequent user of my library's E-book collection.
Entire Sample	32.25%	9.50%	27.25%	27.00%	4.00%

Table 1.2: Students' opinion of college library's E-book collection, Broken Out by Age of the Student

Years of Age	I am not sure what an E-book is.	I don't think that my library has an E-book collection.	My library has E-books but I never use them.	I use the library E-book collection occasionally.	I'm a frequent user of my library's E-book collection.
19 or younger	37.82%	10.90%	25.00%	21.79%	4.49%
20-21	28.57%	6.77%	27.07%	31.58%	6.02%
22-24	34.38%	3.13%	34.38%	28.13%	0.00%
25-30	29.55%	15.91%	22.73%	29.55%	2.27%
over 30	24.00%	12.00%	36.00%	28.00%	0.00%

Table 1.3: Students' opinion of college library's E-book collection, Broken Out by Population Intensity of the Place of Origin

Population Intensity of Place of Origin of the Student	I am not sure what an E-book is.	I don't think that my library has an E-book collection.	My library has E-books but I never use them.	I use the library E-book collection occasionally.	I'm a frequent user of my library's E-book collection.
City with more than 350,000	34.16%	6.83%	27.33%	25.47%	6.21%
Small or Medium Sized City with less than 350,000	31.40%	9.92%	25.62%	29.75%	3.31%
Suburban Area	22.73%	18.18%	31.82%	22.73%	4.55%
Rural Area	32.98%	11.70%	27.66%	26.60%	1.06%

**Table 1.4:   Students' opinion of college library's E-book collection,
Broken Out by Geographic Region of Origin of the Student**

Region of the Country Where the Student Grew Up	I am not sure what an E-book is.	I don't think that my library has an E-book collection.	My library has E-books but I never use them.	I use the library E-book collection occasionally.	I'm a frequent user of my library's E-book collection.
South	32.77%	8.09%	26.81%	28.51%	3.83%
Northeast	35.19%	11.11%	26.85%	24.07%	2.78%
Midwest	16.67%	50.00%	16.67%	16.67%	0.00%
West	27.03%	10.81%	35.14%	18.92%	8.11%

**Table 1.5:   Students' opinion of college library's E-book collection,
Freshmen, Sophomores, Juniors & Seniors**

Year or Grade in School	I am not sure what an E-book is.	I don't think that my library has an E-book collection.	My library has E-books but I never use them.	I use the library E-book collection occasionally.	I'm a frequent user of my library's E-book collection.
Freshmen	38.33%	7.49%	25.99%	23.79%	4.41%
Sophomores	26.87%	13.43%	31.34%	23.88%	4.48%
Juniors	20.00%	20.00%	40.00%	10.00%	10.00%
Seniors	23.16%	10.53%	25.26%	38.95%	2.11%

**Table 1.6:   Students' opinion of college library's E-book collection,
Broken Out by Broken Out by Income Level of the Student's Family of Origin**

Annual Income of Student's Family of Origin	I am not sure what an E-book is.	I don't think that my library has an E-book collection.	My library has E-books but I never use them.	I use the library E-book collection occasionally.	I'm a frequent user of my library's E-book collection.
Less than $40,000	34.10%	7.83%	28.57%	26.73%	2.76%
$40,00 to $75,000	34.13%	14.29%	23.02%	26.98%	1.59%
$75,000+ to $150,000	16.67%	0.00%	50.00%	25.00%	8.33%
More than $150,000	21.95%	7.32%	26.83%	26.83%	17.07%

Table 1.7:   Students' opinion of college library's E-book collection, Broken Out by Level of Religiosity of the Student

Level of Religiosity	I am not sure what an E-book is.	I don't think that my library has an E-book collection.	My library has E-books but I never use them.	I use the library E-book collection occasionally.	I'm a frequent user of my library's E-book collection.
I practice a religion thoroughly and consider my religion to be a very important part of my life.	32.52%	6.80%	28.16%	29.61%	2.91%
I practice a religion and try to attend regular services and to participate as much a I can.	39.77%	7.95%	26.14%	19.32%	6.82%
I identify with a religion but can't say I put a lot of effort into practicing it.	35.29%	17.65%	41.18%	5.88%	0.00%
I don't really believe in or practice an organized religion.	24.42%	16.28%	23.26%	32.56%	3.49%

Table 1.8:   Students' opinion of college library's E-book collection, Broken Out by The Political Views of the Student

Political Views of the Student	I am not sure what an E-book is.	I don't think that my library has an E-book collection.	My library has E-books but I never use them.	I use the library E-book collection occasionally.	I'm a frequent user of my library's E-book collection.
Very Left Wing	34.29%	9.29%	27.14%	26.43%	2.86%
Liberal	34.92%	10.32%	24.60%	26.19%	3.97%
Middle of the Road	12.50%	6.25%	43.75%	37.50%	0.00%
Conservative	29.25%	9.43%	27.36%	28.30%	5.66%
Very Right Wing	33.33%	8.33%	33.33%	16.67%	8.33%

Table 1.9:   Students' opinion of college library's E-book collection, Broken Out by Grade Point Average or Equivalent

Grades of the Student	I am not sure what an E-book is.	I don't think that my library has an E-book collection.	My library has E-books but I never use them.	I use the library E-book collection occasionally.	I'm a frequent user of my library's E-book collection.
A- or Better	29.90%	8.76%	29.90%	28.35%	3.09%
B- to B+	35.18%	8.54%	25.13%	26.13%	5.03%
C- to C+	0.00%	66.67%	0.00%	33.33%	0.00%
D or Less	25.00%	50.00%	25.00%	0.00%	0.00%

Table 1.10: Students' opinion of college library's E-book collection, Broken Out by Academic Major or Focus

Major or Focus	I am not sure what an E-book is.	I don't think that my library has an E-book collection.	My library has E-books but I never use them.	I use the library E-book collection occasionally.	I'm a frequent user of my library's E-book collection.
Business, Economics, Finance, Engineering, Math	33.75%	8.75%	27.50%	26.88%	3.13%
Fine or Performing Arts	40.54%	10.81%	21.62%	21.62%	5.41%
Hard Sciences	29.73%	17.57%	27.03%	24.32%	1.35%
Education	40.00%	0.00%	32.00%	20.00%	8.00%
English, Communications, Languages or Journalism	27.27%	13.64%	22.73%	27.27%	9.09%
Social Sciences	28.77%	5.48%	27.40%	34.25%	4.11%

Table 1.11: Students' opinion of college library's E-book collection, Broken Out by Gender of the Student

Gender of the Student	I am not sure what an E-book is.	I don't think that my library has an E-book collection.	My library has E-books but I never use them.	I use the library E-book collection occasionally.	I'm a frequent user of my library's E-book collection.
Male	29.25%	7.48%	32.65%	27.89%	2.72%
Female	33.99%	10.67%	24.11%	26.48%	4.74%

Table 1.12:   Students' opinion of college library's E-book collection, Broken Out by Public and Private College Students

Attends Public or Private College	I am not sure what an E-book is.	I don't think that my library has an E-book collection.	My library has E-books but I never use them.	I use the library E-book collection occasionally.	I'm a frequent user of my library's E-book collection.
Attends Public College	33.79%	8.97%	27.59%	26.55%	3.10%
Attends Private College	28.44%	11.01%	26.61%	28.44%	5.50%

Table 1.13:   Students' opinion of college library's E-book collection, Broken Out by Type of College Living Arrangement

Living Arrangement of the Student	I am not sure what an E-book is.	I don't think that my library has an E-book collection.	My library has E-books but I never use them.	I use the library E-book collection occasionally.	I'm a frequent user of my library's E-book collection.
At home with my parents or guardian	34.18%	10.13%	24.05%	27.22%	4.43%
Off campus with others who are not my parents or guardian	34.48%	7.76%	30.17%	24.14%	3.45%
Off campus alone	20.00%	20.00%	40.00%	20.00%	0.00%
In Fraternity or Sorority Supplied Housing	66.67%	0.00%	16.67%	16.67%	0.00%
On campus in the dorms or college-provided suites	26.09%	10.43%	28.70%	30.43%	4.35%

Table 1.14: Students' opinion of college library's E-book collection, Broken Out by Student Employment Situation

Student Employment Situation	I am not sure what an E-book is.	I don't think that my library has an E-book collection.	My library has E-books but I never use them.	I use the library E-book collection occasionally.	I'm a frequent user of my library's E-book collection.
Doesn't Have a Full or Part Time Job	31.31%	8.59%	26.26%	29.80%	4.04%
Has a Part Time Job	33.33%	9.60%	28.79%	24.24%	4.04%
Has a Full Time Job	25.00%	50.00%	0.00%	25.00%	0.00%

Table 1.15: Students' opinion of college library's E-book collection, Broken Out by Type of College

Type of College	I am not sure what an E-book is.	I don't think that my library has an E-book collection.	My library has E-books but I never use them.	I use the library E-book collection occasionally.	I'm a frequent user of my library's E-book collection.
Community College	37.18%	8.97%	28.21%	23.08%	2.56%
BA-Level	27.03%	16.22%	21.62%	32.43%	2.70%
MA-Level	35.63%	11.49%	22.99%	26.44%	3.45%
PHD Level	36.78%	5.75%	29.89%	20.69%	6.90%
Research University	25.47%	7.55%	30.19%	33.02%	3.77%

Table 1.16: Students' opinion of college library's E-book collection, Broken Out by Size of Enrollment of College

Total Enrollment of College Attended by the Student	I am not sure what an E-book is.	I don't think that my library has an E-book collection.	My library has E-books but I never use them.	I use the library E-book collection occasionally.	I'm a frequent user of my library's E-book collection.
Less than 2,000	21.15%	19.23%	21.15%	38.46%	0.00%
2000-5000	32.88%	9.59%	36.99%	19.18%	1.37%
5001-10,000	41.43%	7.14%	21.43%	24.29%	5.71%
10.001-25,000	32.41%	6.48%	28.70%	26.85%	5.56%
More than 25,000	31.11%	7.78%	26.67%	28.89%	5.56%

Table 1.17:   Students' opinion of college library's E-book collection, Broken Out by Publicly Claimed Mean SAT Acceptance Score of the College Attended

Mean SAT Acceptance Score of College Attended by Student	I am not sure what an E-book is.	I don't think that my library has an E-book collection.	My library has E-books but I never use them.	I use the library E-book collection occasionally.	I'm a frequent user of my library's E-book collection.
less than 1500	36.03%	8.09%	26.47%	27.21%	2.21%
1500 to 1649	29.27%	11.38%	27.64%	28.46%	3.25%
1650 to 1799	31.48%	5.56%	29.63%	25.00%	8.33%
1800 to 1950	44.44%	5.56%	22.22%	27.78%	0.00%
More than 1950	16.67%	25.00%	25.00%	33.33%	0.00%

QUESTON #2: Students Rating of College Library E-book Collection's Accessibility & Ease of Use

Table 2.1: Students' rating of college library E-book collection's accessibility

	Very easy to access and use	Relatively easy to access and use	Moderately difficult to access and use	Very difficult to access and use	I'm not really sure
Entire Sample	10.83%	24.94%	8.31%	0.76%	55.16%

Table 2.2: Students' rating of college library E-book collection's accessibility, Broken Out by Age of the Student

Years of Age	Very easy to access and use	Relatively easy to access and use	Moderately difficult to access and use	Very difficult to access and use	I'm not really sure
19 or younger	8.28%	22.29%	5.10%	1.91%	62.42%
20-21	12.21%	29.01%	12.21%	0.00%	46.56%
22-24	12.50%	25.00%	3.13%	0.00%	59.38%
25-30	9.30%	30.23%	6.98%	0.00%	53.49%
over 30	16.67%	12.50%	16.67%	0.00%	54.17%

Table 2.3: Students' rating of college library E-book collection's accessibility, Broken Out by Population Intensity of the Place of Origin

Population Intensity of Place of Origin of the Student	Very easy to access and use	Relatively easy to access and use	Moderately difficult to access and use	Very difficult to access and use	I'm not really sure
City with more than 350,000	13.13%	21.88%	11.25%	0.63%	53.13%
Small or Medium Sized City with less than 350,000	13.33%	25.83%	5.00%	0.83%	55.00%
Suburban Area	9.09%	31.82%	9.09%	0.00%	50.00%
Rural Area	4.30%	25.81%	7.53%	1.08%	61.29%

Table 2.4:   Students' rating of college library E-book collection's accessibility, Broken Out by Geographic Region of Origin of the Student

Region of the Country Where the Student Grew Up	Very easy to access and use	Relatively easy to access and use	Moderately difficult to access and use	Very difficult to access and use	I'm not really sure
South	12.39%	22.65%	8.12%	0.85%	55.98%
Northeast	9.26%	26.85%	7.41%	0.93%	55.56%
Midwest	0.00%	33.33%	0.00%	0.00%	66.67%
West	8.33%	25.00%	8.33%	0.00%	58.33%

Table 2.5:   Students' rating of college library E-book collection's accessibility, Broken Out by Freshmen, Sophomores, Juniors & Seniors

Year or Grade in School	Very easy to access and use	Relatively easy to access and use	Moderately difficult to access and use	Very difficult to access and use	I'm not really sure
Freshmen	10.67%	24.00%	7.11%	1.33%	56.89%
Sophomores	8.96%	23.88%	2.99%	0.00%	64.18%
Juniors	10.00%	0.00%	20.00%	0.00%	70.00%
Seniors	12.77%	30.85%	13.83%	0.00%	42.55%

Table 2.6:   Students' rating of college library E-book collection's accessibility, Broken Out by Broken Out by Income Level of the Student's Family of Origin

Annual Income of Student's Family of Origin	Very easy to access and use	Relatively easy to access and use	Moderately difficult to access and use	Very difficult to access and use	I'm not really sure
Less than $40,000	9.81%	24.77%	8.41%	0.93%	56.07%
$40,00 to $75,000	11.11%	20.63%	7.94%	0.79%	59.52%
$75,000+ to $150,000	8.33%	50.00%	0.00%	0.00%	41.67%
More than $150,000	15.00%	32.50%	10.00%	0.00%	42.50%

Table 2.7:   Students' rating of college library E-book collection's accessibility, Broken Out by Level of Religiosity of the Student

Level of Religiosity	Very easy to access and use	Relatively easy to access and use	Moderately difficult to access and use	Very difficult to access and use	I'm not really sure
I practice a religion thoroughly and consider my religion to be a very important part of my life.	10.84%	26.60%	7.39%	1.48%	53.69%
I practice a religion and try to attend regular services and to participate as much a I can.	10.11%	19.10%	10.11%	0.00%	60.67%
I identify with a religion but can't say I put a lot of effort into practicing it.	5.88%	17.65%	5.88%	0.00%	70.59%
I don't really believe in or practice an organized religion.	10.59%	29.41%	8.24%	0.00%	51.76%

Table 2.8:   Students' rating of college library E-book collection's accessibility, Broken Out by the Political Views of the Student

Political Views of the Student	Very easy to access and use	Relatively easy to access and use	Moderately difficult to access and use	Very difficult to access and use	I'm not really sure
Very Left Wing	12.23%	23.02%	8.63%	0.72%	55.40%
Liberal	7.14%	27.78%	9.52%	0.00%	55.56%
Middle of the Road	12.50%	43.75%	12.50%	0.00%	31.25%
Conservative	11.65%	24.27%	4.85%	1.94%	57.28%
Very Right Wing	25.00%	0.00%	16.67%	0.00%	58.33%

Table 2.9:   Students' rating of college library E-book collection's accessibility, Broken Out by Grade Point Average or Equivalent

Grades of the Student	Very easy to access and use	Relatively easy to access and use	Moderately difficult to access and use	Very difficult to access and use	I'm not really sure
A- or Better	9.84%	24.87%	10.88%	1.55%	52.85%
B- to B+	12.18%	24.87%	6.09%	0.00%	56.85%
C- to C+	0.00%	33.33%	0.00%	0.00%	66.67%
D or Less	0.00%	25.00%	0.00%	0.00%	75.00%

Table 2.10: Students' rating of college library E-book collection's accessibility, Broken Out by Academic Major or Focus

Major or Focus	Very easy to access and use	Relatively easy to access and use	Moderately difficult to access and use	Very difficult to access and use	I'm not really sure
Business, Economics, Finance, Engineering, Math	10.19%	25.48%	7.01%	0.64%	56.69%
Fine or Performing Arts	8.11%	27.03%	2.70%	5.41%	56.76%
Hard Sciences	15.07%	23.29%	6.85%	0.00%	54.79%
Education	4.00%	16.00%	12.00%	0.00%	68.00%
English, Communications, Languages or Journalism	4.55%	22.73%	18.18%	0.00%	54.55%
Social Sciences	10.81%	28.38%	10.81%	0.00%	50.00%

Table 2.11: Students' rating of college library E-book collection's accessibility, Broken Out by Gender of the Student

Gender of the Student	Very easy to access and use	Relatively easy to access and use	Moderately difficult to access and use	Very difficult to access and use	I'm not really sure
Male	13.10%	26.21%	10.34%	0.69%	49.66%
Female	9.52%	24.21%	7.14%	0.79%	58.33%

Table 2.12: Students' rating of college library E-book collection's accessibility, Broken Out by Public and Private College Students

Attends Public or Private College	Very easy to access and use	Relatively easy to access and use	Moderately difficult to access and use	Very difficult to access and use	I'm not really sure
Attends Public College	10.80%	23.00%	8.71%	1.05%	56.45%
Attends Private College	10.09%	30.28%	7.34%	0.00%	52.29%

Table 2.13: Students' rating of college library E-book collection's accessibility, Broken Out by Type of College Living Arrangement

Living Arrangement of the Student	Very easy to access and use	Relatively easy to access and use	Moderately difficult to access and use	Very difficult to access and use	I'm not really sure
At home with my parents or guardian	10.76%	22.78%	8.86%	1.27%	56.33%
Off campus with others who are not my parents or guardian	10.53%	23.68%	7.02%	0.88%	57.89%
Off campus alone	0.00%	0.00%	40.00%	0.00%	60.00%
In Fraternity or Sorority Supplied Housing	0.00%	33.33%	0.00%	0.00%	66.67%
On campus in the dorms or college-provided suites	12.28%	29.82%	7.89%	0.00%	50.00%

Table 2.14: Students' rating of college library E-book collection's accessibility, Broken Out by Student Employment Situation

Student Employment Situation	Very easy to access and use	Relatively easy to access and use	Moderately difficult to access and use	Very difficult to access and use	I'm not really sure
Doesn't Have a Full or Part Time Job	10.71%	30.10%	6.12%	0.51%	52.55%
Has a Part Time Job	11.17%	19.80%	10.66%	1.02%	57.36%
Has a Full Time Job	0.00%	25.00%	0.00%	0.00%	75.00%

Table 2.15: Students' rating of college library E-book collection's accessibility, Broken Out by Type of College

Type of College	Very easy to access and use	Relatively easy to access and use	Moderately difficult to access and use	Very difficult to access and use	I'm not really sure
Community College	8.97%	19.23%	6.41%	3.85%	61.54%
BA-Level	8.11%	29.73%	5.41%	0.00%	56.76%
MA-Level	10.23%	22.73%	5.68%	0.00%	61.36%
PHD Level	13.10%	21.43%	8.33%	0.00%	57.14%
Research University	12.38%	32.38%	12.38%	0.00%	42.86%

Table 2.16: Students' rating of college library E-book collection's accessibility, Broken Out by Size of Enrollment of College

Total Enrollment of College Attended by the Student	Very easy to access and use	Relatively easy to access and use	Moderately difficult to access and use	Very difficult to access and use	I'm not really sure
Less than 2,000	9.62%	32.69%	5.77%	0.00%	51.92%
2000-5000	6.85%	26.03%	6.85%	0.00%	60.27%
5001-10,000	11.59%	24.64%	2.90%	0.00%	60.87%
10.001-25,000	16.04%	18.87%	12.26%	1.89%	50.94%
More than 25,000	8.89%	27.78%	10.00%	0.00%	53.33%

Table 2.17:   Students' rating of college library E-book collection's accessibility, Broken Out by Publicly Claimed Mean SAT Acceptance Score of the College Attended

Mean SAT Acceptance Score of College Attended by Student	Very easy to access and use	Relatively easy to access and use	Moderately difficult to access and use	Very difficult to access and use	I'm not really sure
less than 1500	9.63%	21.48%	7.41%	2.22%	59.26%
1500 to 1649	13.93%	22.13%	7.38%	0.00%	56.56%
1650 to 1799	9.35%	31.78%	10.28%	0.00%	48.60%
1800 to 1950	5.56%	33.33%	5.56%	0.00%	55.56%
More than 1950	16.67%	25.00%	16.67%	0.00%	41.67%

QUESTION #3: Percentage of students who have ever received any form of in or out of class training from a college librarian in how to use the college library E-book collection

Table 3.1: Percentage of students who have ever received any form of in or out of class training from a college librarian in how to use the college library E-book collection

	Yes	No
Entire Sample	30.42%	69.58%

Table 3.2: Percentage of students who have ever received any form of in or out of class training from a college librarian in how to use the college library E-book collection, Broken Out by Age of the Student

Years of Age	Yes	No
19 or younger	29.49%	70.51%
20-21	35.34%	64.66%
22-24	28.13%	71.88%
25-30	29.55%	70.45%
over 30	24.00%	76.00%

Table 3.3: Percentage of students who have ever received any form of in or out of class training from a college librarian in how to use the college library E-book collection, Broken Out by Population Intensity of the Place of Origin

Population Intensity of Place of Origin of the Student	Yes	No
City with more than 350,000	34.57%	65.43%
Small or Medium Sized City with less than 350,000	30.58%	69.42%
Suburban Area	13.64%	86.36%
Rural Area	25.53%	74.47%

Table 3.4: Percentage of students who have ever received any form of in or out of class training from a college librarian in how to use the college library E-book collection, Broken Out by Geographic Region of Origin of the Student

Region of the Country Where the Student Grew Up	Yes	No
South	32.34%	67.66%
Northeast	33.03%	66.97%
Midwest	16.67%	83.33%
West	16.22%	83.78%

Table 3.5: Percentage of students who have ever received any form of in or out of class training from a college librarian in how to use the college library E-book collection, Broken Out by Freshmen, Sophomores, Juniors & Seniors

Year or Grade in School	Yes	No
Freshmen	31.86%	68.14%
Sophomores	26.09%	73.91%
Juniors	20.00%	80.00%
Seniors	31.58%	68.42%

Table 3.6: Percentage of students who have ever received any form of in or out of class training from a college librarian in how to use the college library E-book collection, Broken Out by Broken Out by Income Level of the Student's Family of Origin

Annual Income of Student's Family of Origin	Yes	No
Less than $40,000	30.88%	69.12%
$40,00 to $75,000	29.37%	70.63%
$75,000+ to $150,000	25.00%	75.00%
More than $150,000	36.59%	63.41%

Table 3.7: Percentage of students who have ever received any form of in or out of class training from a college librarian in how to use the college library E-book collection, Broken Out by Level of Religiosity of the Student

Level of Religiosity	Yes	No
I practice a religion thoroughly and consider my religion to be a very important part of my life.	31.55%	68.45%
I practice a religion and try to attend regular services and to participate as much a I can.	25.84%	74.16%
I identify with a religion but can't say I put a lot of effort into practicing it.	11.76%	88.24%
I don't really believe in or practice an organized religion.	34.88%	65.12%

Table 3.8: Percentage of students who have ever received any form of in or out of class training from a college librarian in how to use the college library E-book collection, Broken Out by the Political Views of the Student

Political Views of the Student	Yes	No
Very Left Wing	25.90%	74.10%
Liberal	29.69%	70.31%
Middle of the Road	37.50%	62.50%
Conservative	37.14%	62.86%
Very Right Wing	25.00%	75.00%

Table 3.9: Percentage of students who have ever received any form of in or out of class training from a college librarian in how to use the college library E-book collection, Broken Out by Grade Point Average or Equivalent

Grades of the Student	Yes	No
A- or Better	28.21%	71.79%
B- to B+	33.67%	66.33%
C- to C+	0.00%	100.00%
D or Less	0.00%	100.00%

Table 3.10: Percentage of students who have ever received any form of in or out of class training from a college librarian in how to use the college library E-book collection, Broken Out by Academic Major or Focus

Major or Focus	Yes	No
Business, Economics, Finance, Engineering, Math	28.13%	71.88%
Fine or Performing Arts	32.43%	67.57%
Hard Sciences	28.38%	71.62%
Education	28.00%	72.00%
English, Communications, Languages or Journalism	50.00%	50.00%
Social Sciences	29.73%	70.27%

Table 3.11: Percentage of students who have ever received any form of in or out of class training from a college librarian in how to use the college library E-book collection, Broken Out by Gender of the Student

Gender of the Student	Yes	No
Male	34.01%	65.99%
Female	28.35%	71.65%

Table 3.12: Percentage of students who have ever received any form of in or out of class training from a college librarian in how to use the college library E-book collection, Broken Out by Public and Private College Students

Attends Public or Private College	Yes	No
Attends Public College	26.55%	73.45%
Attends Private College	40.00%	60.00%

Table 3.13: Percentage of students who have ever received any form of in or out of class training from a college librarian in how to use the college library E-book collection, Broken Out by Type of College Living Arrangement

Living Arrangement of the Student	Yes	No
At home with my parents or guardian	31.01%	68.99%
Off campus with others who are not my parents or guardian	23.73%	76.27%
Off campus alone	0.00%	100.00%
In Fraternity or Sorority Supplied Housing	50.00%	50.00%
On campus in the dorms or college-provided suites	36.84%	63.16%

Table 3.14: Percentage of students who have ever received any form of in or out of class training from a college librarian in how to use the college library E-book collection, Broken Out by Student Employment Situation

Student Employment Situation	Yes	No
Doesn't Have a Full or Part Time Job	31.50%	68.50%
Has a Part Time Job	29.95%	70.05%
Has a Full Time Job	0.00%	100.00%

Table 3.15: Percentage of students who have ever received any form of in or out of class training from a college librarian in how to use the college library E-book collection, Broken Out by Type of College

Type of College	Yes	No
Community College	29.49%	70.51%
BA-Level	27.03%	72.97%
MA-Level	35.96%	64.04%
PHD Level	24.42%	75.58%
Research University	32.08%	67.92%

Table 3.16: Percentage of students who have ever received any form of in or out of class training from a college librarian in how to use the college library E-book collection, Broken Out by Size of Enrollment of College

Total Enrollment of College Attended by the Student	Yes	No
Less than 2,000	32.69%	67.31%
2000-5000	32.43%	67.57%
5001-10,000	25.35%	74.65%
10.001-25,000	34.91%	65.09%
More than 25,000	26.37%	73.63%

Table 3.17: Percentage of students who have ever received any form of in or out of class training from a college librarian in how to use the college library E-book collection, Broken Out by Publicly Claimed Mean SAT Acceptance Score of the College Attended

Mean SAT Acceptance Score of College Attended by Student	Yes	No
less than 1500	30.37%	69.63%
1500 to 1649	32.00%	68.00%
1650 to 1799	31.48%	68.52%
1800 to 1950	27.78%	72.22%
More than 1950	16.67%	83.33%

Question #4: Students' Rating of College Ebook Collection as a Reference or Research Tool

Table 4.1: Students' rating of college E-book collection as a reference or research tool

	Not useful to me	Slightly useful to me	Somewhat useful to me	Useful to me	Very useful to me
Entire Sample	33.52%	17.05%	24.43%	21.31%	3.69%

Table 4.2: Students' rating of college E-book collection as a reference or research tool, Broken Out by Age of the Student

Years of Age	Not useful to me	Slightly useful to me	Somewhat useful to me	Useful to me	Very useful to me
19 or younger	32.85%	21.17%	25.55%	13.87%	6.57%
20-21	35.54%	12.40%	26.45%	23.97%	1.65%
22-24	41.38%	20.69%	13.79%	20.69%	3.45%
25-30	27.78%	19.44%	19.44%	30.56%	2.78%
over 30	31.58%	10.53%	26.32%	31.58%	0.00%

Table 4.3: Students' rating of college E-book collection as a reference or research tool, Broken Out by Population Intensity of the Place of Origin

Population Intensity of Place of Origin of the Student	Not useful to me	Slightly useful to me	Somewhat useful to me	Useful to me	Very useful to me
City with more than 350,000	30.28%	16.90%	25.35%	23.24%	4.23%
Small or Medium Sized City with less than 350,000	34.29%	17.14%	22.86%	22.86%	2.86%
Suburban Area	36.84%	21.05%	21.05%	15.79%	5.26%
Rural Area	38.10%	15.48%	26.19%	16.67%	3.57%

Table 4.4: Students' rating of college E-book collection as a reference or research tool, Broken Out by Geographic Region of Origin of the Student

Region of the Country Where the Student Grew Up	Not useful to me	Slightly useful to me	Somewhat useful to me	Useful to me	Very useful to me
South	34.60%	18.01%	22.27%	21.33%	3.79%
Northeast	32.26%	13.98%	27.96%	22.58%	3.23%
Midwest	50.00%	16.67%	16.67%	16.67%	0.00%
West	28.57%	14.29%	28.57%	25.00%	3.57%

Table 4.5: Students' rating of college E-book collection as a reference or research tool, Broken Out by Freshmen, Sophomores, Juniors & Seniors

Year or Grade in School	Not useful to me	Slightly useful to me	Somewhat useful to me	Useful to me	Very useful to me
Freshmen	33.67%	16.08%	25.63%	20.60%	4.02%
Sophomores	34.43%	21.31%	19.67%	21.31%	3.28%
Juniors	44.44%	11.11%	22.22%	11.11%	11.11%
Seniors	31.33%	16.87%	25.30%	24.10%	2.41%

Table 4.6: Students' rating of college E-book collection as a reference or research tool, Broken Out by Broken Out by Income Level of the Student's Family of Origin

Annual Income of Student's Family of Origin	Not useful to me	Slightly useful to me	Somewhat useful to me	Useful to me	Very useful to me
Less than $40,000	32.28%	15.87%	26.98%	20.63%	4.23%
$40,00 to $75,000	37.50%	20.54%	19.64%	20.54%	1.79%
$75,000+ to $150,000	33.33%	11.11%	22.22%	22.22%	11.11%
More than $150,000	28.95%	15.79%	26.32%	23.68%	5.26%

Table 4.7: Students' rating of college E-book collection as a reference or research tool, Broken Out by Level of Religiosity of the Student

Level of Religiosity	Not useful to me	Slightly useful to me	Somewhat useful to me	Useful to me	Very useful to me
I practice a religion thoroughly and consider my religion to be a very important part of my life.	29.44%	19.44%	26.11%	21.67%	3.33%
I practice a religion and try to attend regular services and to participate as much a I can.	44.30%	13.92%	20.25%	16.46%	5.06%
I identify with a religion but can't say I put a lot of effort into practicing it.	50.00%	7.14%	28.57%	14.29%	0.00%
I don't really believe in or practice an organized religion.	30.26%	17.11%	23.68%	25.00%	3.95%

Table 4.8: Students' rating of college E-book collection as a reference or research tool, Broken Out by the Political Views of the Student

Political Views of the Student	Not useful to me	Slightly useful to me	Somewhat useful to me	Useful to me	Very useful to me
Very Left Wing	29.51%	10.66%	31.15%	24.59%	4.10%
Liberal	36.61%	20.54%	23.21%	16.07%	3.57%
Middle of the Road	20.00%	33.33%	26.67%	20.00%	0.00%
Conservative	38.30%	17.02%	18.09%	24.47%	2.13%
Very Right Wing	22.22%	33.33%	11.11%	11.11%	22.22%

Table 4.9: Students' rating of college E-book collection as a reference or research tool, Broken Out by Grade Point Average or Equivalent

Grades of the Student	Not useful to me	Slightly useful to me	Somewhat useful to me	Useful to me	Very useful to me
A- or Better	54.76%	19.05%	1.19%	20.83%	4.17%
B- to B+	56.25%	14.77%	3.98%	21.59%	3.41%
C- to C+	66.67%	0.00%	0.00%	33.33%	0.00%
D or Less	50.00%	25.00%	0.00%	25.00%	0.00%

Table 4.10: Students' rating of college E-book collection as a reference or research tool, Broken Out by Academic Major or Focus

Major or Focus	Not useful to me	Slightly useful to me	Somewhat useful to me	Useful to me	Very useful to me
Business, Economics, Finance, Engineering, Math	32.62%	19.15%	24.11%	21.99%	2.13%
Fine or Performing Arts	40.63%	25.00%	25.00%	9.38%	0.00%
Hard Sciences	37.68%	14.49%	21.74%	18.84%	7.25%
Education	42.11%	15.79%	26.32%	15.79%	0.00%
English, Communications, Languages or Journalism	37.50%	12.50%	18.75%	25.00%	6.25%
Social Sciences	25.37%	14.93%	28.36%	28.36%	2.99%

Table 4.11: Students' rating of college E-book collection as a reference or research tool, Broken Out by Gender of the Student

Gender of the Student	Not useful to me	Slightly useful to me	Somewhat useful to me	Useful to me	Very useful to me
Male	29.55%	21.97%	25.00%	20.45%	3.03%
Female	35.91%	14.09%	24.09%	21.82%	4.09%

Table 4.12: Students' rating of college E-book collection as a reference or research tool, Broken Out by Public and Private College Students

Attends Public or Private College	Not useful to me	Slightly useful to me	Somewhat useful to me	Useful to me	Very useful to me
Attends Public College	35.04%	16.54%	25.59%	20.08%	2.76%
Attends Private College	29.90%	18.56%	21.65%	23.71%	6.19%

Table 4.13: Students' rating of college E-book collection as a reference or research tool, Broken Out by Type of College Living Arrangement

Living Arrangement of the Student	Not useful to me	Slightly useful to me	Somewhat useful to me	Useful to me	Very useful to me
At home with my parents or guardian	37.06%	15.38%	27.27%	17.48%	2.80%
Off campus with others who are not my parents or guardian	35.05%	18.56%	17.53%	27.84%	1.03%
Off campus alone	25.00%	25.00%	50.00%	0.00%	0.00%
In Fraternity or Sorority Supplied Housing	66.67%	0.00%	0.00%	33.33%	0.00%
On campus in the dorms or college-provided suites	26.67%	18.10%	26.67%	20.95%	7.62%

Table 4.14: Students' rating of college E-book collection as a reference or research tool, Broken Out by Student Employment Situation

Student Employment Situation	Not useful to me	Slightly useful to me	Somewhat useful to me	Useful to me	Very useful to me
Doesn't Have a Full or Part Time Job	26.16%	17.44%	27.91%	26.16%	2.33%
Has a Part Time Job	40.34%	15.91%	21.59%	17.05%	5.11%
Has a Full Time Job	50.00%	50.00%	0.00%	0.00%	0.00%

Table 4.15: Students' rating of college E-book collection as a reference or research tool, Broken Out by Type of College

Type of College	Not useful to me	Slightly useful to me	Somewhat useful to me	Useful to me	Very useful to me
Community College	42.25%	19.72%	21.13%	14.08%	2.82%
BA-Level	30.30%	18.18%	24.24%	27.27%	0.00%
MA-Level	33.33%	14.10%	29.49%	17.95%	5.13%
PHD Level	41.89%	14.86%	16.22%	22.97%	4.05%
Research University	22.58%	18.28%	30.11%	24.73%	4.30%

Table 4.16: Students' rating of college E-book collection as a reference or research tool, Broken Out by Size of Enrollment of College

Total Enrollment of College Attended by the Student	Not useful to me	Slightly useful to me	Somewhat useful to me	Useful to me	Very useful to me
Less than 2,000	33.33%	12.50%	22.92%	27.08%	4.17%
2000-5000	31.15%	19.67%	26.23%	18.03%	4.92%
5001-10,000	38.71%	19.35%	24.19%	16.13%	1.61%
10.001-25,000	32.98%	17.02%	23.40%	21.28%	5.32%
More than 25,000	32.93%	15.85%	25.61%	23.17%	2.44%

Table 4.17: Students' rating of college E-book collection as a reference or research tool, Broken Out by Publicly Claimed Mean SAT Acceptance Score of the College Attended

Mean SAT Acceptance Score of College Attended by Student	Not useful to me	Slightly useful to me	Somewhat useful to me	Useful to me	Very useful to me
less than 1500	33.61%	16.81%	28.57%	17.65%	3.36%
1500 to 1649	37.84%	14.41%	18.92%	24.32%	4.50%
1650 to 1799	28.42%	23.16%	23.16%	21.05%	4.21%
1800 to 1950	37.50%	6.25%	31.25%	25.00%	0.00%
More than 1950	27.27%	9.09%	36.36%	27.27%	0.00%

OTHER REPORTS FROM PRIMARY RESEARCH GROUP INC.

THE SURVEY OF AMERICAN COLLEGE STUDENTS: USE OF DISTANCE EDUCATION
March 2009   Price: view our website at www.PrimaryResearch.com

This report presents more than 100 tables of data exploring how full time college students in the United States view distance learning, how many such courses that they have taken and plan to take, and how they view their level of preparedness for DL courses. The report also presents data on how students view DL courses compared to traditional courses and how many study in colleges that offer DL courses. The data in the report is based on a representative sample of more than 400 full time college students in the United States. Data is broken out by 16 criteria including gender, grade point average, major field of study, income level of students and type, size of college, and mean SAT acceptance score of colleges, among other variables. The report is designed to give college administrators, educational researchers and others benchmarks on student use of distance learning and the student demographics of DL use and future use.

THE SURVEY OF AMERICAN COLLEGE STUDENTS: USE OF & SATISFACTION WITH COLLEGE TUTORING SERVICES
March 2009   Price: view our website at www.PrimaryResearch.com

The report presents 85 tables of data exploring how full time college students in the United States view and use their college's tutoring programs. The data in the report is based on a representative sample of more than 400 full time college students in the United States. Data is broken out by 16 criteria including gender, grade point average, major field of study, income level of students and type, size of college, and mean SAT acceptance score of colleges, among other variables. The report is designed to give college administrators, educational researchers and others benchmarks on the use of college tutoring service against which to compare their own programs or data.

THE INTERNATIONAL SURVEY OF LIBRARY & MUSEUM DIGITIZATION PROJECTS
ISBN: 1-57440-105-X   Price: $89.50   October 2008
The International Survey of Library & Museum Digitization Projects presents detailed data about the management and development of a broad range of library special collection and museum digitization projects. Data are broken out by type of digitization project (i.e., text, photograph, film, audio, etc.) size and type of institution, annual spending on digitization and other variables. The report presents data and narrative on staffing, training, funding, technology selection, outsourcing, permissions and copyright clearance, cataloging, digital asset management, software and applications selection, marketing and many other issues of interest to libraries and museums that are digitizing aspects of their collections.

THE SURVEY OF ACADEMIC & RESEARCH LIBRARY JOURNAL PURCHASING PRACTICES
ISBN: 1-57440-108-4   Price: $89.50   November 2008

This report looks closely at the acquisition practices for scientific, technical and academic journals of academic and research libraries. Some of the many issues covered: attitudes toward the pricing and digital access policies of select major journals publishers, preferences for print, print/electronic access combinations, and electronic access alone arrangements. Covers spending plans, preferences for use of consortiums, and use of, and evaluation of subscription agents. Charts attitudes toward CLOCKSS, open access, use of URL resolvers and other pressing issues of interest to major purchasers of academic and technical journals.

ACADEMIC LIBRARY CATALOGING PRACTICES BENCHMARKS
ISBN: 1-57440-106-8   Price: $89.50   November 2008

This 254-page report presents data from a survey of the cataloging practices of approximately 80 North American academic libraries. In more than 630 tables of data and related commentary from participating librarians and our analysts, the report gives a broad overview of academic library cataloging practices related to outsourcing, selection and deployment of personnel, salaries, the state of continuing education in cataloging, and much more. Data are broken out by size and type of college and for public and private colleges. Survey participants also discuss how they define the cataloger's range of responsibilities, how they train their catalogers, how they assess cataloging quality, whether they use cataloging quotas or other measures to spur productivity, what software and other cataloging technology they use and why, how they make outsourcing decisions and more.

SURVEY OF ACADEMIC LIBRARY USE OF INSTRUCTIONAL TECHNOLOGY:
ISBN: 1-57440-107-6   Price: $85.00   October 2008

The Survey of Academic Library Use of Instructional Technology examines use of information literacy computer labs, classroom response "clicker" technology, whiteboards, and many other educational technologies used by libraries. In an era in which library education has become an increasingly important part of the academic librarian's duties, this report provides insights on how peer institutions are allocating their educational budgets and choosing the most effective technologies and practices in information and general library literacy.

CORPORATE LIBRARY BENCHMARKS, 2009 Edition
ISBN 1-57440-109-2   Publication Date: December 2008 Price: $195.00

Corporate Library Benchmarks, 2009 Edition presents extensive data from 52 corporate and other business-oriented libraries; data is broken out by company size, type of industry and other criteria.

The mean number of employees for the organizations in the sample is 16,000; the median, 1700. Some of the many issues covered in the report are: spending on electronic and print forms of books, directories, journals and other information resources; library staffing trends, number of library locations maintained and the allocation of office space to the library, disputes with publishers, allocation of library staff time, level of awareness of database contract terms of peer institutions, reference workload, and the overall level of influence of the library in corporate decision making.

LIBRARY USE OF E-BOOKS
ISBN: 1-57440-101-7   Price: $75.00   Publication Date: April 2008
Data in the report are based on a survey of 75 academic, public and special libraries. Data are broken out by library budget size, for U.S. and non-U.S. libraries and for academic and non-academic libraries. The report presents more than 300 tables of data on E-book use by libraries, as well as analysis and commentary. Librarians detail their plans on how they plan to develop their E-book collections, what they think of E-book readers and software, and which E-book aggregators and publishers appeal to them most and why. Other issues covered include: library production of E-books and collection digitization, e-book collection information literacy efforts, use of E-books in course reserves and inter-library loan, E-book pricing and inflation issues, acquisition sources and strategies for e-books and other issues of concern to libraries and book publishers.

LAW LIBRARY BENCHMARKS, 2008-09 EDITION
ISBN: 1-57440-104-1   Price: $129.00   Publication Date: October 2008
Data in the report are based on a survey of 55 North American law libraries drawn from law firm, private company, university, courthouse and government agency law libraries. Data are broken out by size and type of library for ease in benchmarking. The 120+ page report covers developments in staffing, salaries, budgets, materials spending, use of blogs & wikis, use of legal directories, the library role in knowledge management, records management and content management systems. Patron and librarian training, reimbursement for library-related education and other issues are also covered in this latest edition.

RESEARCH LIBRARY INTERNATIONAL BENCHMARKS
ISBN: 1-57440-103-3   Publication Date: June 2008   Price: $95.00
Research Library International Benchmarks presents data from a survey of 45 major research libraries from the U.S., Australia, Canada, Spain, the U.K., Japan and others. Data are presented separately for university, government/non-profit and corporate/legal libraries, and for U.S. and non-U.S. libraries, as well as by size of library and type of library, corporate/legal, university and government. The 200-page report presents a broad range of data on current and planned materials, salary, info technology and capital spending, hiring plans, spending trends for E-books, journals, books and much, much more. Provides data on trends in discount margins from vendors, relations with consortiums, information literacy efforts, workstation, laptop and learning space development, use of scanners and digital cameras, use of RFID technology, federated

search and many other pressing issues for major research libraries, university and otherwise.

THE SURVEY OF LIBRARY DATABASE LICENSING PRACTICES
ISBN: 1-57440-093-2   Price: $80.00   Publication Date: December 2007

The study presents data from 90 libraries – corporate, legal, college, public, state and nonprofit libraries – about their database licensing practices. More than half of the participating libraries are from the U.S., and the rest are from Canada, Australia, the U.K. and other countries. Data are broken out by library type and size of library, as well as for overall level of database expenditure. The 100+-page study, with more than 400 tables and charts, presents benchmarking data enabling librarians to compare their library's practices to peers in many areas related to licensing. Metrics provided include: percentage of licenses from consortiums, spending on consortium dues, time spent seeking new consortium partners, number of consortium memberships maintained; growth rate in the percentage of licenses obtained through consortiums; expectation for consortium purchases in the future; number of licenses, growth rate in the number of licenses, spending on licenses for directories, electronic journals, E-books and magazine/newspaper databases; future spending plans on all of the above; price inflation experienced for electronic resources in business, medical, humanities, financial, market research, social sciences and many other information categories; price inflation for F-books, electronic directories, journals and newspaper/magazine databases; percentage of licenses that require passwords; percentage of licenses that have simultaneous access restrictions; spending on legal services related to licenses; and much more.

THE INTERNATIONAL SURVEY OF INSTITUTIONAL DIGITAL REPOSITORIES
ISBN: 1-57440-090-8   Price: $89.50   Publication Date: November 2007

The study presents data from 56 institutional digital repositories from 11 countries, including the U.S., Canada, Australia, Germany, South Africa, India, Turkey and other countries. The 121-page study presents more than 300 tables of data and commentary and is based on data from higher education libraries and other institutions involved in institutional digital repository development. In more than 300 tables and associated commentary, the report describes norms and benchmarks for budgets, software use, manpower needs and deployment, financing, usage, marketing and other facets of the management of international digital repositories. The report helps to answer questions such as: who contributes to the repositories and on what terms? Who uses the repositories? What do they contain and how fast are they growing in terms of content and end use? What measures have repositories used to gain faculty and other researcher participation? How successful have these methods been? How has the repository been marketed and cataloged? What has been the financial impact? Data are broken out by size and type of institution for easier benchmarking.

PREVAILING & BEST PRACTICES IN ELECTRONIC AND PRINT SERIALS MANAGEMENT
ISBN: 1-57440-076-2   Price: $80.00   Publication Date: November 2005

This report looks closely at the electronic and print serials procurement and management practices of 11 libraries, including: the University of Ohio, Villanova University, the Colorado School of Mines, Carleton College, Northwestern University, Baylor University, Princeton University, the University of Pennsylvania, the University of San Francisco, Embry-Riddle Aeronautical University and the University of Nebraska Medical Center. The report looks at both electronic and print serials and includes discussions of the following issues: selection and management of serials agents, including the negotiation of payment; allocating the serials budget by department; resolving access issues with publishers; use of consortiums in journal licensing; invoice reconciliation and payment; periodicals binding, claims, check-in and management; serials department staff size and range of responsibilities; serials management software; use of open access archives and university depositories; policies on gift subscriptions, free trials and academic exchanges of publications; use of electronic serials/catalog linking technology; acquisition of usage statistics; cooperative arrangements with other local libraries and other issues in serials management.

CORPORATE LIBRARY BENCHMARKS, 2007 Edition
ISBN: 1-57440-084-3   Price: $189.00

This report, our sixth survey of corporate libraries, presents a broad range of data, broken out by size and type of organization. Among the issues covered are: spending trends on books, magazines, journals, databases, CD-ROMs, directories and other information vehicles, plans to augment or reduce the scope and size of the corporate library, hiring plans, salary spending and personnel use, librarian research priorities by type of subject matter, policies on information literacy and library education, library relations with management, budget trends, breakdown in spending by the library versus other corporate departments that procure information, librarian use of blogs and RSS feeds, level of discounts received from book jobbers, use of subscription agents, and other issues of concern to corporate and other business librarians.

EMERGING ISSUES IN ACADEMIC LIBRARY CATALOGING & TECHNICAL SERVICES
ISBN: 1-57440-086-X   Price: $72.50   Publication Date: April 2007

This report presents nine highly detailed case studies of leading university cataloging and technical service departments. It provides insights into how they are handling 10 major changes facing them, including: the encouragement of cataloging productivity; impact of new technologies on and enhancement of online catalogs; the transition to metadata standards; the cataloging of Websites and digital and other special collections; library catalog and metadata training; database maintenance, holdings and physical processing; managing the relationship with acquisitions departments; staff education; and other important issues. Survey participants represent academic libraries of varying sizes and classifications, with many different viewpoints. Universities surveyed are: Brigham Young; Curry College; Haverford College; Illinois, Louisiana and Pennsylvania State

Universities; University of North Dakota; University of Washington; and Yale University.

THE MARKETING OF HISTORIC SITES, MUSEUMS, EXHIBITS AND ARCHIVES
ISBN: 1-57440-074-6   Price: $95.00   Publication Date: June 2005

This report looks closely at how history is presented and marketed by organizations such as history museums, libraries, historical societies, and historic sites and monuments. The report profiles the efforts of the Vermont Historical Society, Hook's Historic Drug Store and Pharmacy, the Thomas Jefferson Foundation/Monticello, the Musee Conti Wax Museum of New Orleans, the Bostonian Society, the Dittrick Medical History Center, the Band Museum, the Belmont Mansion, the Kansas State Historical Society, the Computer History Museum, the Atari Virtual Museum, the Museum of American Financial History, the Atlanta History Center and the public libraries of Denver and Evansville. The study's revealing profiles, based on extensive interviews with executive directors and marketing managers of the institutions cited, provide a deeply detailed look at how history museums, sites, societies and monuments are marketing themselves.

LICENSING AND COPYRIGHT MANAGEMENT: BEST PRACTICES OF COLLEGE, SPECIAL AND RESEARCH LIBRARIES
ISBN: 1-57440-068-1   Price: $80 Publication Date: May 2004

This report looks closely at the licensing and copyright-management strategies of a sample of leading research, college and special libraries and consortiums and includes interviews with leading experts. The focus is on electronic-database licensing, and includes discussions of the most pressing issues: development of consortiums and group buying initiatives, terms of access, liability for infringement, archiving, training and development, free-trial periods, contract language, contract-management software and time-management issues, acquiring and using usage statistics, elimination of duplication, enhancement of bargaining power, open-access publishing policies, interruption-of-service contingency arrangements, changes in pricing over the life of the contract, interlibrary loan of electronic files, copyright clearance, negotiating tactics, uses of consortiums, and many other issues. The report profiles the emergence of consortiums and group-buying arrangements.

TRENDS IN TRAINING COLLEGE FACULTY, STUDENTS & STAFF IN COMPUTER LITERACY
ISBN: 1-57440-085-1   Price: $67.50   Publication Date: April 2007

This report looks closely at how nine institutions of higher education are approaching the question of training faculty, staff and students in the use of educationally oriented information technologies. The report helps answer questions such as: what is the most productive way to help faculty master new information technologies? How much should be spent on such training? What are the best practices? How should distance learning instructors be trained? How formal, and how ad-hoc, should training efforts be? What should computer literacy standards be among students? How can subject-specific computer literacy be integrated into curriculums? Should colleges develop their own training methods, buy packaged solutions, find them on the Web?

Organizations profiled are: Brooklyn Law School, Florida State University College of Medicine, Indiana University Southeast, Texas Christian University, Clemson University, the Teaching & Learning Technology Group, the Appalachian College Association, Tuskegee Institute and the University of West Georgia.

THE SURVEY OF LIBRARY CAFÉS
ISBN: 1-57440-089-4   Price: $75.00   Publication Date: 2007
The Survey of Library Cafés presents data from more than 40 academic and public libraries about their cafés and other foodservice operations. The 60-page report gives extensive data and commentary on library café sales volume, best-selling products, impacts on library maintenance costs, reasons for starting a café, effects on library traffic, and many other issues regarding the decision to start and manage a library café.